CREATIVE SOULS

COLOR, WORDS, AND SPIRIT

CREATIVE SOULS

COLOR, WORDS, AND SPIRIT

By Larry P. Morris

Art by Vonda K. Drees

LPM Publications
Kirkland, WA

Copyright © 2018 by Larry P. Morris
Illustrations Copyright © 2018 by Vonda K. Drees

All rights reserved. No part of this book may be reproduced, stored in, or introduced into a retrieval system, or transmitted in any form, or by any means (electronic, mechanical, photocopying, records, or otherwise) without the prior written permission of the authors.

ISBN-13: 978-1983616969
INSBN-10: 1983616966

Editor: Julie Scandora

Art: Vonda K. Drees

Scripture quotations are from the New Revised Standard Version of the Bible, copyright @1989, Division of Christian Education of the National Council of Churches of Christ in the United States of America. Used by permission. All rights reserved.

For additional copies of this book, check at your local bookstore or on Amazon. This book is also available in e-versions.

To those who create

Contents

Introduction 1
Drink Deeply 2
       Let Water be the Sacred Sign, illustration

Suffering Servants 4
       God is Present in the Oppressed, illustration

Pray On 6
       When You Pray Move Your Feet, illustration

At the Foot of the Mountain 8
       And the Mountain Top Comes to Us, illustration

Lost in Worship 10
       A Moment of Grace, illustration

Where My Soul Can Breathe 12
       Beauty Can Connect Our Hearts, illustration

Pray Always 14
       We Become Original, illustration

One Step at a Time 16
       Show up in Love, illustration

Dreamers 18
       What Do You Hope For …, illustration

Silly and Healing 20
    Your Healing Come, illustration

Kyrie Eleison 22
    Kyrie Eleison, Suffering, illustration

Among Us 24
    Alleluia, You Make All Things New, illustration

The Wisdom of Planting Seeds 26
    Be Born in Us, illustration

Becoming Like a Child 28
    The Kingdom of Heaven is within You, illustration

The Simple Things of Ash Wednesday 30
    An Endless Sea, Love, illustration

Come to the Silence 32
    Trusting in the Silence, illustration

All of Our Days 34
    Breathe in God, Breathe out Love, illustration

I Am 36
    I Am, God's Dwelling Place, illustration

The Art of Creation 38
    The Artist's Love, illustration

I Shall Dwell in the House of the Lord Forever 40
    Love Brings Us Home, illustration

Wonder with Me 42
    Trust Your Wonder, illustration

Time to Pray 44
    Prayer, Being Present, One with God, illustration

Baseball Hats, Jesus, and Christmas 46

That All May Be One, illustration

Many Other Signs 48

New Life, Easter, Wonder, illustration

Preparing 50

Awaken, illustration

About the Author and the Artist 53
Spiritual Writers/Speakers quoted in this book 54
Index of Titles, First Lines and Illustrations 55

Introduction

Writing and art are usually solitary activities. Writers and artists go inside of themselves. They listen to their own creative spirit. They listen to the voices of others that echo inside them. And they listen to The Spirit who called them to create in the first place. Out of that journey, from that process, their creative work arises.

Therefore, when the opportunity comes for one creative soul to collaborate with another, a whole new layer of creativity comes into play. Collaboration has the potential to create something greater than the inspiration of each of the individual works. It has the possibility to open doors and show ideas in new ways.

The idea of this collaboration first came as I saw Vonda's illustrations and noticed themes in her work that crossed paths with many of my writings. When I paired a number of my writings and her artwork, showed her the potential, and then asked if she was interested in collaborating, she said "Yes." Then the work and fun began!

It's our hope that you, our readers, will be inspired by the works in the book and by our collaboration with each other and with The Spirit.

> The Spirit calls our hearts and souls
> To love and grace that makes us whole
> To create and find what makes us new
> To collaborate with the Spirit too

Larry P. Morris

Drink Deeply

The water runs over the head and back to the font. "I baptize you . . ."
In that water and in those words love touches us.
The invisible become visible, the intangible becomes tangible,
the universal becomes personal,
"for you".
Life is renewed; we are born a second time.
We are re-created.

Then the water returns to its work.
It runs into the drains and into our streams, into our rivers and into the lakes.
It evaporates into our clouds and gathers into our rain.
It gives life to the plants of the field and fish in the sea,
the birds of the air and to us.

It renews and refreshes. It quenches and gives life.
It comes and it goes
again and again.

Where has this water been that sits in this cup in front of me?
Was it at the beginning
when God separated the dry land from the seas?
Was it there when Moses parted the sea?
Was it there when Jesus was baptized?
Was it there when I was baptized?
Now it sits here in front of me.

The water of life comes again and again
and is calling me to remember God's creation in the beginning
and God's re-creation in me and in you.
Drink deeply.

Suffering Servants

They gather in their holy place on the first day of the week,
and when then they leave, they leave to serve.

They serve with prayers and hugs.
They serve with questions and then listening
to difficult stories and troubling diagnoses.
They serve tending to the gardens and yards
of those who are too sick or too tired or too sad to pull weeds.
They serve with smiles and jokes and at times with tears,
when hearts are joined in love and in pain.
They serve with meals and notes with flowers
and texts with kind words and open hearts.
They serve with love that finds its healing way
to bring light into darkness.
They give of their time.
And their attention.
And their labor.
And their love.

And on the next first day of the week,
they will gather again
in their holy place to worship
and pray and taste love,
for they are the suffering servants of our days,
of our time, of our lives.
They are our neighbors, and they are us.

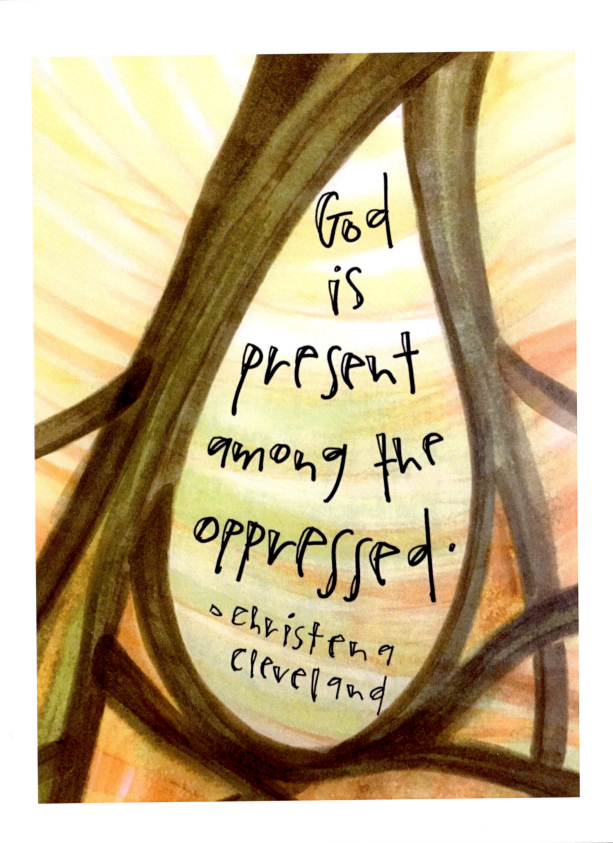

Pray On

She knits as she prays for her friends and family and neighbors.
And perhaps because of her prayers
their lives come together a little, one loop at a time.

He walks as he prays for people he knows who are struggling.
And perhaps the ground under their feet is a bit more firm
and their journey a little more smooth.

She lights a candle as she prays for the conflicts in the world.
And perhaps the light of grace
sees its way here and there among the violence.

He cooks as he prays for those in need.
And perhaps the bread of life feeds one more soul.

She watches the sunset as she prays for those who are alone.
And perhaps their eyes are surprised by the beauty
that has been there all along.

And the prayers of God's people
find their ways into and through our lives and our passions.
And perhaps that is how it was supposed to be.
Pray on.

At the Foot of the Mountain

At the foot of the mountain,
there is a holy place
where the saints of God gather to sing
and pray and hope
and cry out for justice.

At the foot of the mountain,
there is a holy place
where pain is remembered
and sins are forgiven,
where passion is inspired
and eyes are opened,
where the walls are painted with stories for all
and all are surrounded
by the Grace that will see us
to the mountain top.

Till that day,
we gather at the foot of mountain
in that holy place,
and the mountain top
comes to us.

Lost in Worship

She worships nearly every Sunday.
Even though she listens to the lessons
and sings the music,
that's not why she is there.

She comes to worship
to experience a sense of mystery,
and she almost always finds it,
sometimes in the middle of a song,
sometimes in the quiet of the offering,
or sometimes in the simplicity of communion.

When it finds her,
she takes a breath,
often she has a tear,
and she pauses.

She'll catch up to the service in a few minutes,
but for that moment,
she's lost in worship.

Where My Soul Can Breathe

Have you seen the wonderful, vibrant,
colorful moments as the sun sets in the evening?
And have you stopped your whole life to be a part of it?

Have you heard the birds come alive
and sing to the heavens
as the sun comes up in the morning?
And did you stop in wonder to drink it in?

Have you stood in front of a painting
and been so absorbed that nothing else mattered
and you simply smiled?
I have.

In those moments
I was renewed,
I was reborn,
I was gifted.
My soul said yes and breathed deeply again.

So these days,
I stand outside as the sun sets.
I open my windows to hear the birds.
I put my body in the places
where my soul can breathe deeply, again.
"Yes."

Pray Always

On the field, he hits his team's opponents as hard as anyone,
and after the play he helps them up, off the ground.
Pray always.

He makes a six-figure salary and a huge bonus,
working in a downtown tower, and he often gets out at lunch
and eats with a homeless friend, whose name is Frank.
Pray always.

She is a tyrant of a mother,
always reminding her kids of their homework
and making them eat vegetables,
and every week she takes a meal to an unemployed friend
and they eat together, sometimes in tears.
Pray always.

She is a popular student getting great grades.
She studies and studies, knowing that hard work pays off,
and she often confuses her friends
by eating lunch with the unpopular kids and
laughing at their jokes.
Pray always.

All the girls want him as a boyfriend.
He is cute and athletic and thoughtful,
and he tells his girlfriend he has a line he will not cross
for both of their futures.
Pray always.

She's operated a deli for many years and makes tough decisions,
and when a man tells her he lost his wallet
and he didn't know till the meal was ready, she says,
"Eat up and pay tomorrow."
Pray always.

Jesus tells us to *pray always*, so we close eyes
and pray and pray and pray, and the seeds of grace are planted
and grow in our hearts and minds and souls
till the vines find their way into our games and our work,
into our families and friendships, and into all our lives.

And the prayers become hopes.
And the hopes become actions.
And the actions become love.

Pray always.

One Step at a Time

There is in the distance a mountain.
It sits in the haze of the early morning.
It's faint, but it is there and it calls us.
One step after another
and we will make it.
We may need to backtrack from time to time.
We may need to find a better way over the river.
We may need to find an opening through the gully.
But we will do it because it calls us.

Love calls us to the mountain in the distance.
Justice calls us to the mountain in the haze.
Hope keeps us on the trail.

Someday we will reach the Promised Land,
someday we will rest from the work.
Till then, we look into the haze,
we hold onto hope,
and we take one step at time.

Dreamers

"Their heads are in the clouds," they say.
"They're only dreamers," they say.
"Get your feet on the ground," they say.

But I dream on.
I consider what might be,
what should be, what could be,
what we can become.

I dream about
how love could change the world,
how one person could make a difference,
how one community could begin a movement.

I dream from my heart.
I vision from my passion.
I hope inside my prayers.

And I pray that all the dreamers among us,
that those gifted with visions,
will never give up, will always do their work,
till the rest of us see.
Dream on.

Silly and Healing

Once there was a woman who was goofy,
the silly, funny kind of goofy.
She brought a smile to people's lips when she came into a room,
and it was a good bet that laughter was soon to follow.
It came to her naturally.

In her role as a pastor
she had also learned to be strong and compassionate,
especially when she gathered with people grieving
or stood with a family at a death bed
or sat with a couple in trouble.
They knew they could lean on her strength,
and her compassion made it clear they were not alone.

Later, when she was silly again,
those whom she had helped felt the most free to laugh,
and they laughed hard.
After the laughter, it wasn't unusual for them to cry again,
and this time
the tears were healing.

Kyrie Eleison

Kyrie eleison, Lord, have mercy

Old, old words from a distant old world
In an old dead language, on a cold page unfurled

Kyrie eleison, Lord, have mercy

Words of regret, words of sorrow
An act of contrition, a hope for tomorrow

Kyrie eleison, Lord, have mercy

Words spoken for thousands of years
Words cleansed by uncountable tears

Kyrie eleison, Lord, have mercy

Words we utter with barely a sound
Words that free us when we are bound

Kyrie eleison, Lord, have mercy

Words to reclaim, words to hold dear
Love to remember, love to call near

Kyrie eleison, Lord, have mercy

Among Us

The church was full today, and among us were
two felons who have served time,
fourteen people who have committed adultery,
(four of whom think they are the only ones who know)
six who have stolen from their employer,
three who have lied on their resume.

Six who yelled at their kids yesterday,
five who have done illegal drugs in the last month,
sixty-four who don't trust God to provide for them tomorrow,
twenty-eight who lied last week
(sixteen of whom think lying last week was the right thing to do),
twenty-four people who are addicts
(including the six who haven't admitted it yet).

Forty-one people who have not yet forgiven their neighbor,
fifty-seven people who said mean things about someone else last week,
forty-nine people who have not taken care of their 'temple,'
twenty-seven people who are afraid
that something will overwhelm them (really afraid).

Ninety-six people who would like their neighbor's car
or their neighbor's house or job or spouse or kids,
sixty-two people who don't think they have any real gifts to share,
thirty-one people who think they are better than others,
eleven people who share very little of what they have with the church
or with any other group or with any other person.

The church was full today. And we all heard the words,
"With joy, I proclaim to you that Almighty God,
rich in mercy, abundant in love, forgives you all your sin,
and grants you newness of life in Jesus Christ."
And we were all born again, again.

The Wisdom of Planting Seeds

They were farmers by profession
and they taught me the value planting of seeds.

He had grown up on that farm.
When they married, she moved in
and it became a home for both of them.
They knew how to plant and when to do it.
They could read the weather and the soil and they knew the seeds.
They knew it all.

But before they left the house in the morning,
before he went to the fields,
before she went out to the garden and the orchard,
my grandparents would sit at their kitchen table
and read from their Bible and other devotionals books.
They would listen to words of grace and hope,
patience and faith, challenge and forgiveness.
Those words would plant seeds of wisdom and kindness,
courage and faithfulness.

After their prayers, he would pull on his coveralls and an old hat,
she would step into her boots, and they would go out
to read the weather and work the soil and plant the seeds.

And while he cultivated and tilled
and while she harvested the string beans and the apples,
the seeds they had planted that morning would color their thoughts
and would grow in their hearts and souls.

They were farmers by profession
and they taught us the wisdom of planting seeds.

Becoming Like a Child

Once upon a time, there was young girl
who liked to run and paint
and take her boots off to dance in the puddles.

As she grew she learned how to
paint inside the lines and write on the lines
and sit at a desk to learn and read
and memorize and run in a line
and work hard and work together
and compete and win and lose
and celebrate and console.

She graduated at the top of her class
and got a good job and married
and was promoted and had children
and was successful and planted a garden in rows
and retired having accomplished much.

And as she grew old, she heard the words of Jesus
calling her once again "to become like a child."
So she finger-painted with her grandchildren
and she ran, just a bit, sort off.

And one day, all by her herself,
she slipped off her shoes, walked outside,
and danced in the puddles.
It was colder than she remembered
but she did remember and she felt silly and she felt good.

And the kingdom of God is like that, like all of that.

The Simple Things of Ash Wednesday

We go together.
There are hundreds of us.
There are millions of us around the world,
walking to the ashes, to the dust.
We will each hear the words,
"Remember that you are dust and to dust you shall return,"
and the ashes will be smeared on our foreheads
in a simple experience, in an ancient ritual, in a primal sign.

The sign will remind us that we are on a journey.
It will, at best, take us years to arrive.
And the closer we get to the end,
the simpler the journey will become.

We are returning to the dust of the first creation,
the dust of the first creator.
We are returning to the one who made us
from dust and breath and sent us to love.
And when we arrive, we, the people of dust, will find
we have returned to love, simple, endless love.

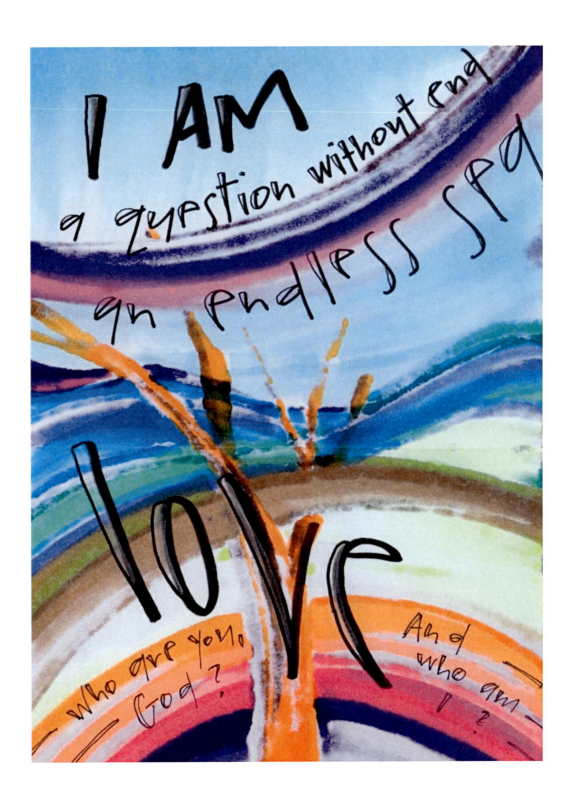

Come to the Silence

To be quiet is a skill.
To let go takes work.

Silence is more than being quiet.
It is more than being alone.

To be silent is to be unoccupied.
It is to not watch, to not read,
to not focus or think or plan.
It is to let go and be in the mystery
of God's love,
of God's presence.

After the busyness
of our mind slows,
after the distractions dim and the voices fade,
we can rest.
We can experience peace.
We can simply be.
And we can know God again.

"Be still and know that I am."
Come to the silence. Come. Be.

Then, when it's time to go,
go in peace to love and to serve.

All of Our Days

When the sounds of the world go quiet
and your breath says, "I am still here,"
When the tasks of life are tomorrow's
and you're at peace in the present, without fear
When you sit in the restful places
and your soul is alone, in good ways
It is then when you see all the wonders
that surround us, all of our days

I Am

Moses asked, "Who shall I tell them has sent me?"
God answered "Tell them I AM has sent you."
Moses did, and we still do.

"I am the beginning and the end.
I was here at creation,
and all things are still made through me.
I am the good shepherd.
I will lead you by still waters
and restore your soul.
I am the women who has lost a coin
and sweeps the house over and over
searching for you.
I am the patient Father giving you freedom
and waiting with a party for your return.
I am the resurrection and the life.
I know pain and separation and death,
and I will never leave you alone in those places.
I am the word of God incarnate, in the flesh.
I have come to be with you,
to join you and to love you.
Because I AM
you are, forever."

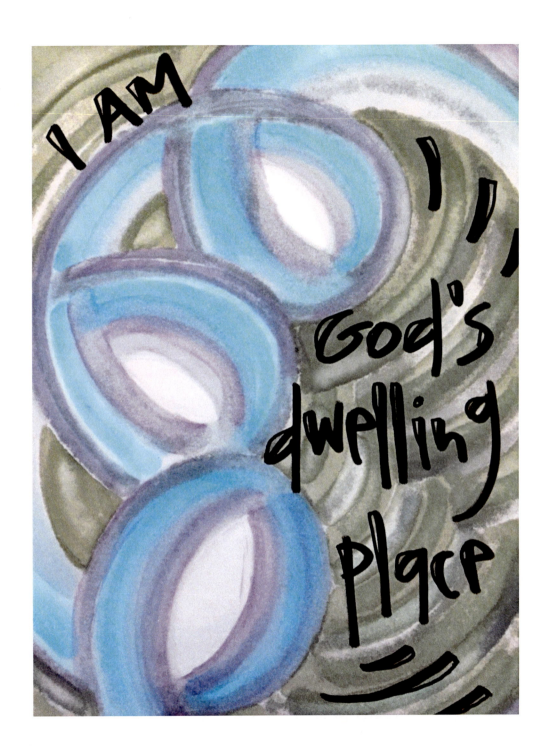

The Art of Creation

A canvas sits on an easel,
next to it a palette with blobs of paint,
and a can of brushes waits
for the artist's vision.

A slab of granite sits on the ground
alongside the chisels and hammer
and anticipates the sculptor's dreams.

The pieces of cloth lie across the table.
Scissors, blades, and a mat
are at the ready,
patient for the quilter's heart.

In the beginning
the Spirit swept over the face of the waters
ready for the work of God.

And the creator's vision
and dreams and heart began to create. . . .

And here you are.

I Shall Dwell in the House of the Lord Forever

When Kristen was an infant, her grandma took care of her some days. At nap time, Grandma would rock her slowly back and forth and would gently whisper the Twenty-Third Psalm, "The Lord is my Shepherd, I shall not want. . . ." By the time she finished, Kristen slept.

When Kristen was five, her parents worked evenings, so Grandma would put her to bed at night. Grandma would sit on the edge of the bed, hold her hand, and quietly say the Twenty-Third Psalm. "The Lord is my shepherd, I shall not want. He makes me lie down in green pastures. . . ." Sometimes Grandma would stop before the end because she thought Kristen had fallen asleep. Kristen would then whisper "More . . . more." Grandma would finish, and Kristen slept.

When Kristen was a senior in college, her mother called and told her that Grandma's cancer was inoperable, that they had moved her to hospice, and that she wouldn't live long. Kristen flew home that day and went immediately to see Grandma. As she stood at the side of the bed, Grandma's breathing was heavy, and her eyes were closed. Kristen had tears and didn't quite know what to say. Finally, she took Grandma's hand and said, "The Lord is my shepherd, I shall not want . . ." When she got to the verse "Even though I walk through the valley of the shadow of death," she stopped and had more tears.

When Kristen paused, Grandma whispered "More . . . more." Kristen's mother took Grandma's other hand, and together, the two women prayed,
    'Even though I walk through the valley of the shadow of death, I fear no evil for you are with me. Your rod and your staff they comfort me. You prepare a table before me in the presence of my enemies, you annoint my head with oil, my cup overflows. Surely goodness and mercy shall follow me all the days of my life, and I shall dwell in the house of the Lord forever.

When they finished, all three women whispered, "Forever, forever," and Grandma slept.

Wonder with Me

Wonder with me at the peaceful blue sky
and the night stars that illumine the darkness.
Wonder with me at the wiggling toes of a newborn child
and the delicate flowers of a tree in bloom.
Wonder with me at a mother's love for her child
and an artist's work to create pure joy
from nothing but paint and paper.
Wonder with me
at the miracle of my breath
and yours,
and all the other simple miracles in our lives.
Wonder with me
and today
let's call those wonderings
"prayers of awe!"
Wonder with me.

Time to Pray

I can pray anytime
and often do
as I drive,
as I walk,
as I work out,
as I play the piano.

But at the end of the day
when my activity slows
and darkness comes
and I am finally quiet,
there is a time
that seems holy.
There is a time when praying seems natural.
There is a time when God's heart
seems available.
Or perhaps it is my heart
that is open.
Either way,
it's time to pray.

Baseball Hats, Jesus, and Christmas

We gathered to worship the Babe in the manger, the one who came for all of us, every one.

I sat behind a young man with a baseball hat on. His mother leaned over and quietly said to him, "Do you see anyone else with a hat on?" He leaned back and mumbled something to her that I didn't understand, but she did. He was clearly developmentally disabled, and she understood his language. He looked to be in his twenties, but his mind was not nearly that old.

He sat down in the middle of hymns when he was bored, and he stood while others sat. He stood when he was distracted or when he was attracted to something.

His parents gently, patiently, brought him back to the proper position as they were able. They held the music for him and followed it with their finger so that he might read and he might stay focused, maybe.

And Jesus came for all of us that night: for those who sang the hymns and responsively read the psalm, for those who sat at the right times and stood when they were supposed to, for those who understood the sermon, and yes, for those with baseball hats who needed gentleness and patience and may have understood things very differently than the rest of us, his brothers and sisters.

Jesus came for all of us that night, every one. Merry Christmas!

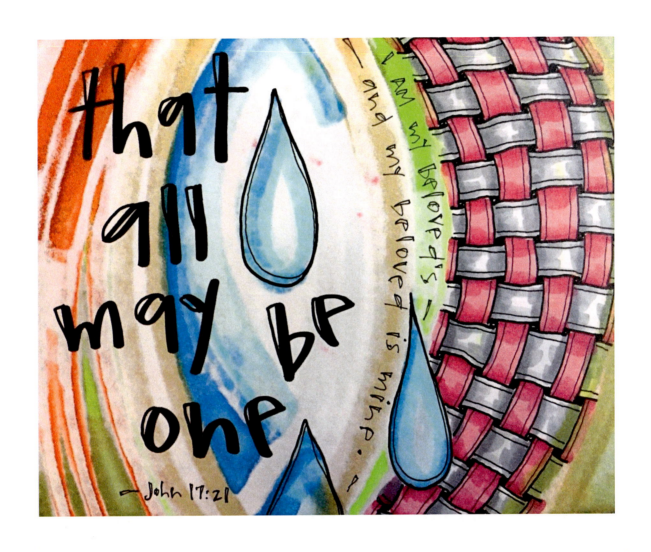

Many Other Signs

We gathered this morning to worship
as we do all Sunday mornings,
with expectation.

We confessed our sin,
fessed up to our pride,
admitted our fear,
and heard words of grace

We were caught up in a sermon of peace,
"The Peace of the Lord," which brings rest
to our frantic lives and gave deep comfort
to a dear sister, who on Easter Sunday
closed her eyes to this world and rose in another.

Then during the special music, a very young girl in a back pew
quietly slipped off her shoes and tiptoed along the wall,
crossed behind the pulpit,
and handed the pastor, her mom, a gift.
They hugged, and with her job finished,
she tiptoed back behind the pulpit,
along the wall, and snuggled up to her dad.
Love and delight touched those who noticed.

Some of the words in today's Gospel told us:
"Now Jesus did many other signs in the presence of his disciples."
Our experience tells us . . . the signs continue.

Preparing

The Bible does not lack
for warning us to prepare.
And it usually involves the threat of judgment.
"But about that day or hour no one knows,
Neither the angels in Heaven, nor the Son, but also the Father.
Keep alert, for you do not know when the time will come."

We leap to believe that God's coming is a threat.
And, in our world
where we believe people should get what they deserve,
where we hope people will get what they deserve,
we both fear and long for judgment.

But perhaps Jesus is also warning us to prepare for grace.
"And what I say to you I say to all: Keep awake."
Jesus told stories of grace and surprise,
of a lost sheep being frantically sought and found,
of a woman desperately searching for one single lost coin,
of a wayward son and patient father.

Perhaps we need to prepare our hearts
for the forgiveness of criminals, for the loving of our enemies,
for the last to be first, for our world to be turned upside down.

Perhaps we need to prepare our eyes
to see Jesus in the powerless, to recognize Jesus in the weak,
to know Jesus in the least of these.

Yes, that must be at least part of what the one
who came in a manger was warning us to prepare for.
Come, Lord Jesus.

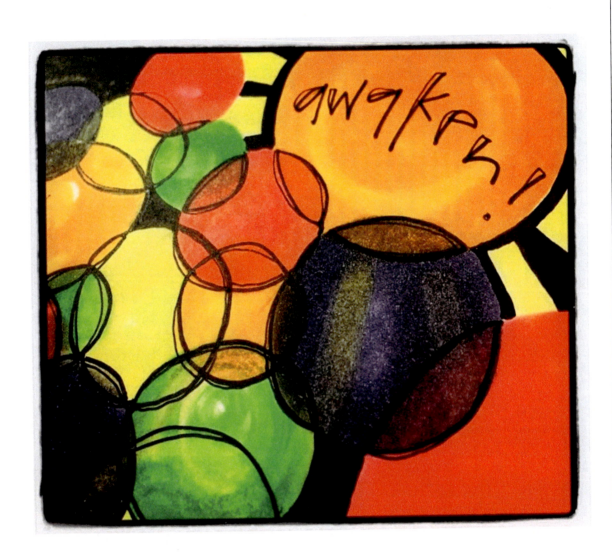

About the Author and the Artist

Larry P. Morris

Larry P. Morris is the author of two books of prose, poetry, and stories. *Among Us: Stories of Worship and Faith* and *Dancing with the Mystery: Stories of Faith, Life, and Cancer*. He is a part-time clergyman at Holy Spirit Lutheran in Kirkland, Washington, and a full-time chief operating officer for a manufacturing company.

He gives readings of his writings around the Pacific Northwest and publishes regularly on his Facebook author page. Larry preaches using his poetry and stories to tell the story of God's love. You may email him at *PlarryMorris@gmail.com*.

Vonda K. Drees

Vonda K. Drees is one of the directors at the Grünewald Guild, a retreat center near Leavenworth, Washington, that welcomes and inspires all who seek to explore the relationships between art, faith, and community. Learn more about the Guild at *https://grunewaldguild.com/*.

She enjoys creating visual imagery as a way to process the Spirit's stirring. Vonda also loves to lead others in this creative process, teaching at the Grünewald Guild and facilitating online journaling groups. Visit *https://vondadrees.com* to see more of her work.

Spiritual Writers/Speakers quoted in this book

Jan Richardson
"Creativity, after all, is God's first language."
Jan Richardson is an artist, writer, and ordained minister in the United Methodist Church. She serves as director of The Wellspring Studio, LLC, and makes her home in Florida. Her books include *Night Visions*, *In the Sanctuary of Women*, and her most recent book, *The Cure for Sorrow: A Book of Blessings for Times of Grief*. janrichardson.com

Christena Cleveland
"God is present among the oppressed."
Christena Cleveland is a social psychologist, public theologian, associate professor of the Practice of Organizational Studies at Duke University's Divinity School, and author of *Disunity in Christ: Uncovering the Hidden Forces that Keep Us Apart*.

Richard Caemmerer
"Beauty can connect our hearts to the Divine Heart."
Richard Caemmerer founded the Grunewald Guild with his wife, Liz, in 1980, after having chaired the Art Department at Valparaiso University and designed hundreds of worship spaces around the world. Richard left this life peacefully on February 16, 2016, with his family at his side. His vision for the church, the guild, and his prolific artwork continues to inspire people all over the world.

Kelly Fryer
"Show up in love. We are called to go deeper than nice."
Kelly Fryer helped launch the mission and leadership program at Luther Seminary, where she served as an assistant professor. She has written more than a dozen books on the topic of mission and leadership, including *Reclaiming the "L" Word: Renewing the Church from its Lutheran Core*.

Seth Godin
"We become original through practice."
Seth Godin is the author of eighteen books that have been bestsellers around the world and have been translated into more than thirty-five languages. He writes about the post-industrial revolution, the way ideas spread, marketing, quitting, leadership, and most of all, changing everything. You might be familiar with his books *Linchpin*, *Tribes*, *The Dip*, and *Purple Cow*.

Index of Titles, First Lines and Illustrations

A canvas sits on an easel, 38

A Moment of Grace, illustration, 11

All of Our Days, 34

Alleluia, You Make All Things New, illustration, 25

Among Us, 24

An Endless Sea, Love, illustration, 31

And The Mountain Top Comes To Us, illustration, 9

At the foot of the mountain, 8

At the Foot of the Mountain, 8

Awaken, illustration, 51

Baseball Hats, Jesus, and Christmas, 46

Be Born In Us, illustration, 27

Beauty Can Connect Our Hearts, illustration, 13

Becoming Like a Child, 28

Breathe in God, Breathe out Love, illustration, 35

Come to the Silence, 32

Dreamers, 18

Drink Deeply, 2

God is Present in the Oppressed, illustration, 5

Have you seen the wonderful, 12

I Am, 36

I Am, God's Dwelling Place, illustration, 37

I can pray anytime, 44

I Shall Dwell in the House of the Lord Forever, 40

Kyrie Eleison, 22

Kyrie eleison, Lord, have mercy, 22

Kyrie Eleison, Suffering, illustration, 23

Let Water be the Sacred Sign, illustration, 3

Lost in Worship, 10

Love Brings Us Home, illustration, 41

Many Other Signs, 48

Moses asked, "Who shall I tell them, 36

New Life, Easter, Wonder, illustration, 49

On the field, he hits, 14

Once there was a woman, 20

Once upon a time, there was young girl, 28

One Step at a Time, 16

Pray Always, 14

Pray On, 6

Prayer, Being Present, One with God, illustration, 45

Preparing, 50

She knits as she prays, 6

She worships nearly every Sunday, 10

Show Up In Love, illustration, 17

Silly and Healing, 20

Suffering Servants, 4

That All May Be One, illustration, 47

The Art of Creation, 38

The Artist's Love, illustration, 39

The Bible does not lack, 50

The church was full today, 24

The Kingdom of Heaven is Within You, illustration, 29

The Simple Things of Ash Wednesday, 30

The water runs over the head, 2

The Wisdom of Planting Seeds, 26

Their heads are in the clouds, 18

There is in the distance, 16

They gather in their holy place, 4

They were farmers by profession, 26

Time to Pray, 44

To be quiet is a skill, 32

Trust Your Wonder, illustration, 43

Trusting in the Silence, illustration, 33

We Become Original, illustration, 15

We gathered this morning to worship, 48

We gathered to worship the Babe, 46

We go together, 30

What Do You Hope For ..., illustration, 19

When Kristen was an infant, 40

When the sounds of the world go quiet, 34

When You Pray Move Your Feet, illustration, 7

Where My Soul Can Breathe, 12

Wonder with Me, 42

Wonder with me at the peaceful, 42

Your Healing Come, illustration, 21

Made in the USA
San Bernardino, CA
25 August 2018